समर्पित - Dedicated

यह पुस्तक मेरे बच्चों, प्रणव और हितेश, को समर्पित है।

This Book is Dedicated to My Kids, Pranav and Hitesh.

: Meenakshi Tyagi

अ

अनार

(Anaar)
(Pomegranate)

**Short Vowel
as sound of 'a' in "arrive"**

आम

(Aam)
(Mango)

Long Vowel
as sound of ' a ' in " army "

इमली

(Imlee)
(Tamarind)

Short Vowel
as sound of 'i' in "kick"

ईख

(Eekh)
(Sugarcane)

Long Vowel
as sound of ' ii ' in " skiing"

(Ulloo)
(Owl)

Short Vowel
as sound of ' u ' in " put"

(Oon)
(Wool)

Long Vowel
as sound of ' oo ' in " soon"

(Aek)
(One)

Short Vowel
as sound of ' a ' in " ray "

(Aenak)
(Eye-Glasses)

Long Vowel
as sound of ' ae ' in " aeroplane"

(Okhlee)
(Pestle)

Short Vowel
as sound of 'o' in "omit"

औ

औरत

(Aurat)
(Lady)

Long Vowel
as sound of 'ow' in "cow"

(Angoor)
(Grapes)

Short Vowel
as sound of ' ung ' in "Sung"

(Namah)
(Namaste)

Long Vowel
as sound of ' ah ' in "Aha"

(Rishi)
(Saint)

Short Vowel
as sound of ' ri ' in "Ring"

स्वर का अभ्यास

(Swar Practice)

Short vowel as sound of 'a' in "arrive"

Long vowel as sound of 'a' in "army"

Short vowel as sound of 'i' in " kick "

Long vowel as sound of 'ii' in "skiing"

**Short vowel
as sound of 'u' in
"put"**

**Long vowel
as sound of 'oo' in
"soon"**

**Short vowel
as sound of 'a' in
"ray"**

**Long vowel
as sound of 'ae' in
"aeroplane"**

Short vowel as sound of 'o' in "omit"

Long vowel as sound of "ow" in "cow"

Short vowel as sound of 'ung' in "sung"

Short vowel as sound of 'ung' in "sung"

Short vowel
as sound of 'ri' in "ring"

अ आ इ ई

उ ऊ ए ऐ

ओ औ अं अः

ऋ

About the Author

Meenakshi is an extremely Passionate and a Young at Heart Educationist.

She **_LOVES_** to Help the Encourage Kids and Adults, both, to go **_beyond_** their limits and learn new ways to explore their inner and outer potential.

As of the writing of this book, she is working as a Para-Professional in the School District of Redlands, California, USA.

She holds a Post-Graduate (Masters) Degree in Computers Application from University of Kurukshetra, India.

Meenakshi has held several positions of high responsibilities in the field of education in University of Kurukshetra, Haryana, India and many other institutes, schools and colleges in India and US.

She is an active educationist and a go-to volunteer in the field of education and community services.

Meenakshi also runs another education program in the field of Mathematics - **_Vedic Mathematics_** - at www.vedicmathmaster.com. This program is dedicated to teaching the Fastest and most efficient Methods to Master Math. This is one of the most sought-after programs in the field of mathematics around the world.

And above all, Meenakshi is a mother of two beautiful and multi-talented kids – Pranav and Hitesh and is a wife to a supportive husband, Sanjiv.

Connect with the Author

My aim with this book is to help you learn the Hindi alphabets Easily and Effortlessly.

I would therefore love to hear your experience(s) with this book.

Email: meenakshi.tyagi@meenakshityagi.com

Phone: (909) 255-1589

धन्यवाद

Thank You